WORLD EXPLORERS

JACQUES COUSTEAU

Kristin Petrie

Checkerboard
Library

An Imprint of Abdo Publishing
abdobooks.com

ABDOBOOKS.COM

Published by Abdo Publishing, a division of ABDO, PO Box 398166, Minneapolis, Minnesota 55439.
Copyright © 2022 by Abdo Consulting Group, Inc. International copyrights reserved in all countries.
No part of this book may be reproduced in any form without written permission from the publisher.
Checkerboard Library™ is a trademark and logo of Abdo Publishing.

Printed in the United States of America, North Mankato, Minnesota
102021
012022

Design and Production: Tamara JM Peterson, Mighty Media, Inc.
Editor: Liz Salzmann
Cover Photograph: Bettmann/Getty Images
Interior Photographs: David Merrett/Flickr, pp. 24–25; ESB Professional/Shutterstock Images, p. 9; Hans Peters/Wikimedia Commons, p. 29 (bottom); John Lindsay/AP Images, p. 11; Kathy Willens/AP Images, p. 27; majeczka/Shutterstock Images, p. 7; MicroOne/Shutterstock Images, pp. 16–17; Northfielder/Flickr, pp. 21, 28 (top); PA Images/Alamy Photo, p. 15; picture-alliance/dpa/AP Images, p. 5; US Navy/Wikimedia Commons, pp. 23, 28 (bottom); US Navy Office of Naval Intelligence/Wikimedia Commons, pp. 12–13; Vlad61/Shutterstock Images, pp. 19, 29 (top); Wikimedia Commons, pp. 10, 26
Design Elements: Joseph Moxon/Flickr (map), Oleg Iatsun/Shutterstock Images (compass rose)

Library of Congress Control Number: 2021942983

Publisher's Cataloging-in-Publication Data
Names: Petrie, Kristin, author.
Title: Jacques Cousteau / by Kristin Petrie
Description: Minneapolis, Minnesota : Abdo Publishing, 2022 | Series: World explorers | Includes online resources and index.
Identifiers: ISBN 9781532197277 (lib. bdg.) | ISBN 9781098219406 (ebook)
Subjects: LCSH: Cousteau, Jacques, 1910-1997--Juvenile literature. | Discovery and exploration--Juvenile literature. | Exploring expeditions--Juvenile literature. | Explorers--Biography--Juvenile literature. | Oceanography--Juvenile literature.
Classification: DDC 970.01--dc23

CONTENTS

JACQUES COUSTEAU 4

CHILDHOOD 6

SCHOOL AND NAVY 8

A NEW CALLING 10

SPYING 12

THE AQUA-LUNG 14

BRILLIANT COLORS 18

THE *CALYPSO* 20

ENVIRONMENTALIST 22

LATER YEARS 24

THE LEGEND 26

TIMELINE 28

GLOSSARY 30

SAYING IT 31

ONLINE RESOURCES 31

INDEX 32

JACQUES COUSTEAU

A young French boy named Jacques Cousteau loved the water. At first, he just loved to swim and play. But soon, his enjoyment grew into something more. He became curious.

Jacques wanted to see what lay under the ocean's surface. But the salt water stung his eyes. And he could only hold his breath for a short time. He wanted to stay under the water longer.

Jacques was determined to overcome these obstacles. His curious nature and talent for invention helped him to do this. Jacques Cousteau was on his way to being the world's most well-known **oceanographer**, **environmentalist**, and filmmaker.

Jacques Cousteau

CHILDHOOD

St.-André-de-Cubzac, France, was the hometown of Daniel and Elizabeth Cousteau. The couple's second son, Jacques-Yves Cousteau, was born there on June 11, 1910. A few weeks later, the family moved to Paris, France.

In Paris, Daniel worked as a legal adviser for an American millionaire, Eugene Higgins. Daniel traveled often for his job. He brought his family on all of his business trips.

Unfortunately, Jacques was often sick. Doctors told the Cousteaus to limit his activity. Higgins disagreed with the doctors. He thought exercise would improve Jacques's health. Higgins suggested that the Cousteaus let Jacques swim.

Jacques loved to swim. He'd always had a fascination with water. He wondered why some things floated. He wanted to know where bubbles came from and how fish breathed. Now, Jacques was able to spend as much time in the water as he liked.

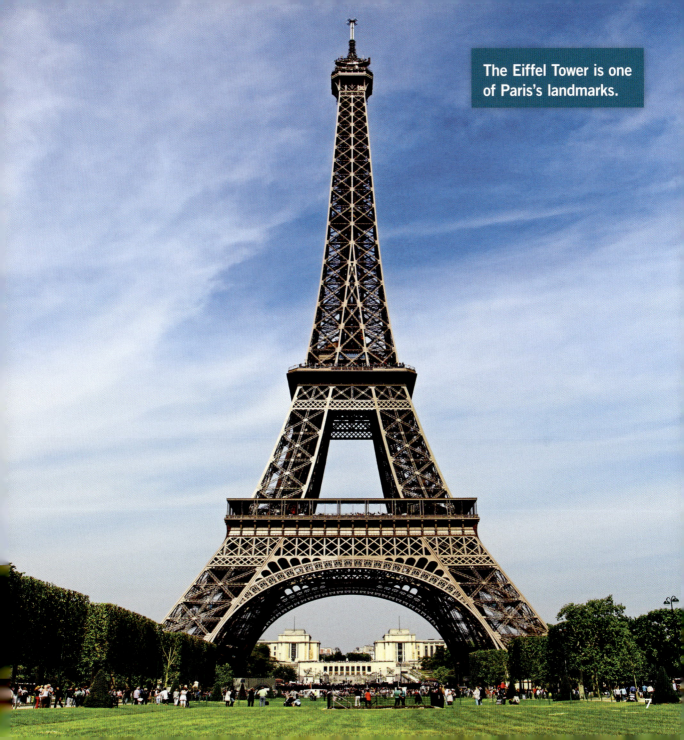
The Eiffel Tower is one of Paris's landmarks.

SCHOOL AND NAVY

As he grew older, Jacques developed a passion for machines. His favorite was the newly invented movie camera. Jacques saved his money and bought one when he was just 13 years old.

Around this time, Jacques lost interest in school. He was considered a poor student and was **expelled** for bad behavior. Eventually, his parents sent him to a **strict** boarding school. Its **discipline** was just what Jacques needed. He graduated at the age of 19.

After graduation, Cousteau joined France's navy. Cousteau studied at a naval **academy** in Brest, France. Then he was stationed at a base in Shanghai, China. From there, he went on **surveying** missions aboard a navy cruiser.

Cousteau decided flying would be his next challenge. So, he entered the navy's **aviation** academy. However, a car accident in 1936 badly damaged his arms. After that, he could not become a pilot. Instead, Cousteau became an instructor at a naval base in Toulon, France.

WOULD YOU?

Would you like to travel around the world with the navy? What do you think Cousteau liked best about this job?

Cousteau was stationed in Shanghai for two years.

A NEW CALLING

Cousteau soon met a lieutenant named Philippe Tailliez. Tailliez advised Cousteau to swim in the Mediterranean Sea to strengthen his arms. Soon, Cousteau and Tailliez met a **civilian** named Frédéric Dumas. The three men shared a love of the ocean and a curiosity about the underwater world.

Philippe Tailliez

Exploring beneath the water's surface became an interest for all three men. They began experimenting with diving and breathing devices. At this time, divers wore heavy iron suits. The suits had hoses that connected divers to their boats so they could receive oxygen. Cousteau wanted to invent a portable breathing machine so divers could move farther from their boats.

Meanwhile, Cousteau met Simone Melchior. She and Cousteau were married on July 12, 1937. The couple had two boys in the following years. Jean-Michel and Philippe both shared their parents' love of the sea and diving.

Cousteau with his wife Simone

SPYING

Cousteau and his friends continued their underwater experiments. Then in 1939, German leader Adolf Hitler sent the German army to invade Poland. This was the beginning of **World War II**. Soon, Italy joined the German forces. France entered the war on Poland's side.

In June 1940, the French navy sent Cousteau to sea on the *Dupleix*. The ship was to sail up the coast and open fire on Genoa, Italy. After completing this assignment, the *Dupleix* safely returned to Toulon. Hitler's army, however, had seized Paris. The French surrendered to the Germans on June 22, 1940.

Cousteau was then assigned to guard duty at a fort near Toulon. There was little military activity at the fort. The Cousteaus had a relatively normal life there.

The *Dupleix* was part of the French Mediterranean war fleet. The fleet was based in Toulon, France, in the 1930s and 1940s.

Secretly, however, Cousteau was still fighting the war. He had joined the French Resistance. This group was working against the German occupation in France. Cousteau's assignments involved underwater spying.

THE AQUA-LUNG

Cousteau's work with the French Resistance increased his determination to invent a better way to dive. He needed to make deeper dives and stay underwater longer. In 1942, Cousteau joined forces with Émile Gagnan in Paris. Gagnan was an engineer and an expert on gas equipment. He and Cousteau developed the Aqua-Lung.

This device had two tanks of **compressed air**, which were worn on a diver's back. Hoses connected the tanks to a mouthpiece. The diver could then breathe the compressed air.

With the Aqua-Lung, Cousteau could dive deep into the water. He didn't have to hurry back to the surface for air. And he was not connected to a boat. So, he was free to roam and explore. Cousteau, Tailliez, and Dumas made hundreds of dives. They tested the limits of the Aqua-Lung.

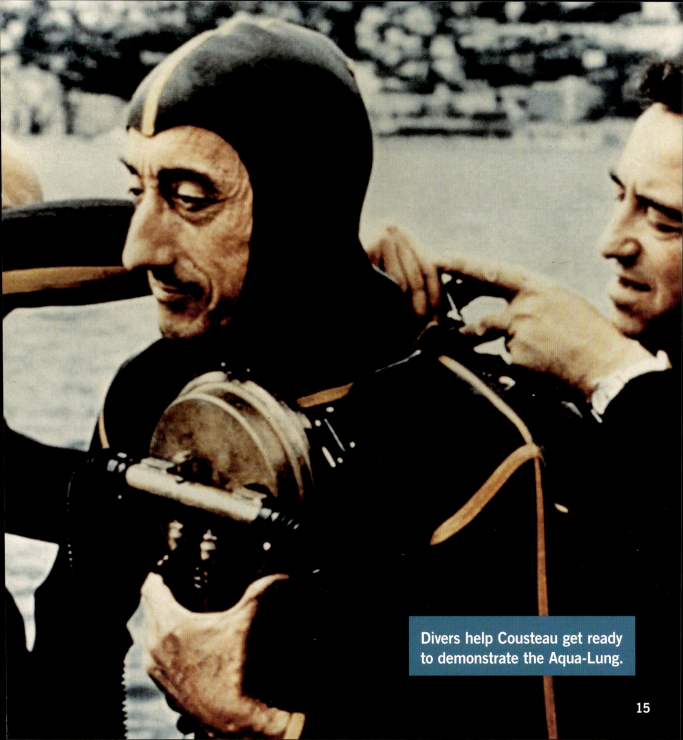

Divers help Cousteau get ready to demonstrate the Aqua-Lung.

BRILLIANT COLORS

Cousteau was one of the first people to bring light to the dark ocean floor. This allowed him and the other divers to see that the ocean was full of brilliant colors. The group took photos and made films of their dives. They improved underwater photography as they went.

In 1942, Cousteau released the film *18 Meters Deep*. This black-and-white movie was the public's first glimpse of the underwater world. Later films included *Danger Under the Sea* and *Landscapes of Silence*. Eventually, Cousteau would make more than 115 films about the ocean.

After the war, Cousteau demonstrated the Aqua-Lung to the navy. He soon received **permission** to begin diving experiments. The navy assigned the Undersea Research Group to Tailliez and Cousteau. The group soon got to work.

EXPLORER EXTRA

The Undersea Research Group had many different assignments. One was to defuse underwater bombs and torpedoes left over from **World War II**. The group also explored sunken ships. As usual, the group recorded all of its work.

Coral reefs show how colorful the ocean floor can be.

19

THE *CALYPSO*

There was much to discover in the underwater world. Cousteau wanted more time to explore. He took a leave of absence from the navy and purchased the *Calypso*. It was a navy ship. Cousteau turned it into a high-tech research vessel.

On November 24, 1951, the *Calypso* set out on its first expedition in the Red Sea. The team included Cousteau, Cousteau's wife, Dumas, and several scientists. During their years of exploring, the group filmed every amazing find. They wanted to share these hidden treasures with the world. They also knew funding for future expeditions would depend on the films they created.

In 1953, Cousteau wrote a book from his ship's logs. It was called *The Silent World*. It was followed with a film of the same name in 1956. This was the first movie Cousteau filmed in color. These accounts of the underwater world made Cousteau famous.

The film *The Silent World* won awards in France and the United States. The French government offered the group financial support. Soon, Cousteau also had support from the National Geographic Society in the United States and other sources.

The *Calypso*

ENVIRONMENTALIST

Cousteau's successful films provided him with the funds to continue inventing. In 1959, Cousteau and his crew developed a diving saucer. The diving saucer was a two-person machine. It could stay underwater for several hours and go 1,148 feet (350 m) below the surface. The diving saucer allowed Cousteau to explore even deeper in the ocean.

In the 1960s, space exploration was reaching new heights. Cousteau set out to prove that humans could live underwater as well as in space. Between 1962 and 1965, "aquanauts" lived in several underwater "houses" for as long as a month!

WOULD YOU?

Would you want to be an aquanaut? What would it be like to live underwater for a month?

Each new device helped develop a better understanding of marine life. Cousteau knew he needed to protect this fragile world. He became a passionate **environmentalist**. Cousteau used television to alert the public to his cause.

In 1968, *The Undersea World of Jacques Cousteau* began airing on television. The show would run for nine years. In 1973, Jacques Cousteau formed the Cousteau Society, which still works to protect marine life.

A crane lifts a diving saucer out of the water.

LATER YEARS

Cousteau continued exploring and diving. His team developed an interest in the rivers that feed the oceans. In 1978, they **surveyed** the Nile River. In 1982 and 1983, Cousteau explored the Amazon River region, and later the Mississippi.

In 1985, Cousteau launched a new ship, the *Alcyone*. That year, the crew set sail on a five-year, around-the-world tour aboard the *Alcyone*. They studied the relationship between people and the ocean.

In 1991, Cousteau began a petition called A Bill of Rights for Future Generations. It addressed the long-term problems of pollution.

Meanwhile, Cousteau experienced changes in his personal life. Sadly, his son Philippe died in 1979 and Simone died of cancer in 1990. The next year, Cousteau married Francine Triplet. The couple had two children named Diane and Pierre-Yves.

The *Alcyone*

THE LEGEND

At the age of 87, Cousteau's amazing career as an **oceanographer** ended. He was hospitalized in Paris for a **respiratory** illness. He was unable to recover. Jacques-Yves Cousteau died on June 25, 1997.

During his lifetime, Cousteau was honored in many ways. France awarded him its highest military award for his work in the French Resistance. US President John F. Kennedy presented him with the National Geographic Society's Special Gold Medal.

The United Nations awarded Cousteau with their International **Environmental** Prize. However, the honor he may have enjoyed most came one year after his death. The United Nations declared 1998 to be the Year of the Ocean.

President John F. Kennedy

WOULD YOU?

Would you give Jacques Cousteau an award? What would it be and why would you give it to him?

Many of Cousteau's awards resulted from his research with the Cousteau Society. Today, the organization has more than 50,000 members working to protect and improve the environment.

TIMELINE

1910
Jacques-Yves Cousteau is born on June 11 in St.-André-de-Cubzac, France.

1951
Cousteau makes his first expedition aboard the *Calypso*.

1942
Cousteau and Gagnan develop the Aqua-Lung. Cousteau makes his first film, *18 Meters Deep*.

1959
Cousteau and his crew develop the diving saucer.

1973

Cousteau forms the Cousteau Society to protect marine life.

1968

The Undersea World of Jacques Cousteau begins airing on television.

1997

Cousteau dies on June 25 in Paris.

GLOSSARY

academy—a private school in which specific subjects are taught.

aviation—having to do with the operation and navigation of aircraft.

civilian—a person who is not a member of the military.

compressed air—a special mixture of breathing gases that are stored in a tank.

discipline—training that teaches order and obedience.

environmental—related to nature and everything in it, such as the land, sea, and air. A person who is concerned about problems of the environment is an environmentalist.

expel—to force out.

oceanographer—an expert in the study of oceans, seas, and marine life.

permission—formal consent.

respiratory—having to do with the system of organs involved with breathing.

strict—severely conforming to a principle or a condition.

survey—to measure a piece of land to determine its shape, area, and boundaries.

World War II—from 1939 to 1945, fought in Europe, Asia, and Africa. Great Britain, France, the United States, the Soviet Union, and their allies were on one side. Germany, Italy, Japan, and their allies were on the other side.

SAYING IT

Émile Gagnan—AY-meel GAH-nyah

Jacques-Yves Cousteau—ZHAHK-EEV koo-STOH

Philippe Tailliez—FEE-leep TEYE-ehz

Shanghai—SHAHNG-HEYE

Toulon—too-LAWN

ONLINE RESOURCES

To learn more about Jacques Cousteau, please visit **abdobooklinks.com** or scan this QR code. These links are routinely monitored and updated to provide the most current information available.

INDEX

Alcyone, 24
Amazon River, 24
Aqua-Lung, 14, 18
aquanauts, 22
awards, 20, 26

Bill of Rights for Future Generations, A, 24
birth, 6

Calypso, 20
childhood, 4, 6, 8
Cousteau Society, 22

Danger Under the Sea, 18
death, 26
diving gear, 10, 14, 18, 22
Dumas, Frédéric, 10, 14, 20
Dupleix, 12

education, 8
18 Meters Deep, 18
environmentalism, 4, 22, 24, 26

family, 6, 8, 10, 12, 20, 24
filmmaking, 4, 8, 18, 20, 22
France, 4, 6, 8, 12, 13, 14, 20, 26
French Resistance, 13, 14, 26

Gagnan, Émile, 14
Germany, 12, 13

health, 6, 8, 10, 26
Higgins, Eugene, 6
Hitler, Adolf, 12

Italy, 12

Kennedy, John F., 26

Landscapes of Silence, 18

military service, 8, 10, 12, 13, 14, 18, 20
Mississippi River, 24

National Geographic Society, 20, 26
Nile River, 24

oceanography, 4, 10, 12, 14, 18, 20, 22, 24, 26

Poland, 12

Red Sea, 20

Silent World, The, 20
swimming, 4, 6, 10

Tailliez, Philippe, 10, 14, 18

Undersea Research Group, 18
Undersea World of Jacques Cousteau, The, 22
United Nations, 26
United States, 20, 24, 26

World War II, 12, 13, 18